CLUB DRUGS

BY CORDELIA T. HAWKINS

CONTENT CONSULTANT
C. MICHAEL WHITE, PHARM.D., FCP, FCCP
DEPARTMENT HEAD & PROFESSOR OF PHARMACY PRACTICE
UNIVERSITY OF CONNECTICUT

Essential Library

An Imprint of Abdo Publishing | abdopublishing.com

ABDOPUBLISHING.COM

Published by Abdo Publishing, a division of ABDO, PO Box 398166, Minneapolis, Minnesota 55439.
Copyright © 2019 by Abdo Consulting Group, Inc. International copyrights reserved in all countries.
No part of this book may be reproduced in any form without written permission from the publisher.
Essential Library™ is a trademark and logo of Abdo Publishing.

Printed in the United States of America, North Mankato, Minnesota
042018
092018

THIS BOOK CONTAINS
RECYCLED MATERIALS

Cover Photo: iStockphoto
Interior Photos: Steve Reigate/Express Newspapers/AP Images, 4–5; Nick Harvey/WireImage/Getty
Images, 8; Shutterstock Images, 11, 13, 27, 30–31, 45, 49, 50–51, 59, 70–71, 79, 81, 95; Rafal Cichawa/
Shutterstock Images, 15; Keystone/AP Images, 16; Scott Houston/Polaris/Newscom, 20; Red Line
Editorial, 24, 48; iStockphoto, 34; LM Otero/AP Images, 36–37; Andrea Delbo/Shutterstock Images,
39; Javier Garcia/Shutterstock Images, 42; US Drug Enforcement Administration, 55; Wave Break
Media/Shutterstock Images, 57; Paul Warner/AP Images, 63; Merja Ojala/AFP/Getty Images, 66;
Monkey Business Images/Shutterstock Images, 69, 84–85; Marius Pirvu/Shutterstock Images, 73; Yui
Mok/Press Association/PA Wire URN:20701659/AP Images, 74; Helene Rogers/Art Directors & TRIP/
Alamy, 76; Fernando Vergara/AP Images, 88; John Luke/The Times/AP Images, 91; Gero Breloer/
Invision/Sony Pictures Entertainment/AP Images, 92–93; Jason DeCrow/AP Images, 96

Editor: Brenda Haugen
Series Designer: Laura Polzin

Library of Congress Control Number: 2017961349

Publisher's Cataloging-in-Publication Data

Names: Hawkins, Cordelia T., author.
Title: Club drugs / by Cordelia T. Hawkins.
Description: Minneapolis, Minnesota : Abdo Publishing, 2019. | Series: Drugs in real life | Includes
        online resources and index.
Identifiers: ISBN 9781532114137 (lib.bdg.) | ISBN 9781532153969 (ebook)
Subjects: LCSH: Designer drugs--Juvenile literature. | Recreational drug use--Juvenile literature. |
        Rave culture--Juvenile literature. | Drug control--United States--Juvenile literature.
Classification: DDC 362.299--dc23

CONTENTS

CLUB DRUGS IN REAL LIFE

As temperatures soared to 92 degrees Fahrenheit (33°C) on July 30, 2016, people thronged the Auto Club Speedway near Fontana, California. The heat couldn't keep away the fans of electronic dance music (EDM) who had come to the Hard Summer rave, an annual music festival. Although the rave was a celebration of EDM, it was also well known for the widespread use of drugs among attendees. Only the year before, two college students had died of overdoses during the festival.

Among the 147,000 people at the 2016 Hard Summer was 22-year-old Derek Lee, a recent college graduate.[1] Derek reportedly took half of a pill of

3,4-methylenedioxymethamphetamine (MDMA), better known as ecstasy, around nine o'clock that evening. Thirty minutes later, he popped the other half. Soon after, he suffered a seizure. Paramedics flew him to a nearby hospital. There, doctors found Derek's body temperature had climbed to 104.8 degrees Fahrenheit (40.4°C). They were unable to revive Derek, who was declared dead at 12:02 a.m.

Meanwhile, 21-year-old San Diego State student Alyssa Dominguez had swallowed an ecstasy pill around five o'clock that evening. She took another at nine o'clock. She seemed fine until it was time to leave. As she sat in the back of a friend's car waiting to exit the parking lot, Alyssa became restless. She began to ramble, but her words didn't make sense. Around two o'clock in the morning, she collapsed with no pulse. Her friends pulled her from the car and began performing cardiopulmonary resuscitation (CPR). They called paramedics, but it was too late. Alyssa was pronounced dead at the hospital.

Despite the two deaths, the festival continued. On July 31,

MUSIC FESTIVALS

Electronic dance music festivals are popular places for drug use. These events feature loud noise, light displays, and plenty of people enjoying the music and dancing. People take hallucinogens and MDMA to intensify the experience. Festivals can occur at arenas and outdoor venues, allowing for even more people to attend. Some festivals last several days. Because of the number of people who attend, it can be impossible to watch for and prevent all drug use.

Roxanne Ngo, a 22-year-old public policy student, attended the rave. Like Derek and Alyssa, Roxanne took ecstasy. Soon after, she suffered a seizure and cardiac arrest. At the hospital, her body temperature registered 104 degrees Fahrenheit (40°C). Despite doctors' efforts to bring her temperature down, Roxanne again went into cardiac arrest. She died around three o'clock in the morning.

ARTHUR'S STORY

On July 14, 2015, Arthur Cave, son of Australian pop star Nick Cave, met a friend on a high, open clifftop near Brighton, England. A talented drummer, the 15-year-old boy had also had a role in the 2014 movie *20,000 Days on Earth* with his father. But today, Arthur had something other than music and acting in mind. He and his friend had decided to try the drug lysergic acid diethylamide (LSD) for the first time. After researching the drug online, they determined that a wide-open space would be the safest place to try it. Although both still had doubts about the drug's possible effects, they took their first dose sometime that afternoon. At first, both seemed fine.

"We've seen (drug deaths at raves) around the nation . . . in L.A., it popped up in Chicago, in San Francisco, in New York. There's something about these events that leads to this rampant drug abuse . . . and young adults are really getting hurt and paying the price."[2]

—Dr. Marc Futernick, emergency services medical director, Dignity Health California Hospital Medical Center, Los Angeles

But as they took another dose, the two boys became confused and disoriented. According to Detective Constable Vicky Lift, Arthur's friend reported having "vivid hallucinations and his thoughts became darker. [The boy] became paranoid and felt like people were staring at him in cars. He couldn't feel what was real and what wasn't real any more."[3]

The friends decided to go home. But Arthur couldn't find his way. He texted a friend: "Where am I? Where am I?" Motorists nearby saw him zigzagging as he walked across the grass at the edge of the cliff. Moments later, he climbed over a safety fence and plunged over the cliffside. It was a 60-foot (18 m) fall. Arthur suffered broken legs, a fractured skull, and bleeding in the brain. Although bystanders attempted to perform CPR, the boy could not be saved.

MONTANA'S STORY

A top student and star athlete, 15-year-old Montana Sean Brown seemed to have the perfect life. But he had begun to dabble in drugs after being prescribed the powerful painkillers morphine and hydrocodone following a tubing accident. Curious about the way the drugs made him feel, Montana next experimented with marijuana. Even being caught by his father—who began to give him random drug tests—didn't stop him.

LSD breaks down when exposed to strong light.

One night, Montana's parents were out of town, leaving him alone with his older brothers Rory and Jack. The three boys invited over their friend Steven, who brought a supply of what he thought was LSD. As soon as they took the drugs, the three brothers became so ill that they had to be rushed to the emergency room. Doctors discovered that instead of LSD, they had taken N-methoxybenzyl-methoxyphenylethylamine (25I-NBOMe), a synthetic drug made to mimic the effects of LSD. But instead of causing the hallucinations LSD is known for, the drug killed Montana. Although his brothers survived, they were left feeling the guilt of Montana's death. As his brother Rory wrote, "I wanted to be that older brother that was always there for you. I would've done anything for you. . . . But now you're gone and I can't." Three people, including the boys' friend Steven, were arrested in connection with the case.[4]

NBOME

In the early 2000s, the drug NBOMe appeared on the illicit market. NBOMe is a synthetic drug similar in structure to MDMA. It is often sold as LSD but is much more powerful. Even a tiny amount can cause a user to have a seizure, experience a heart attack, or stop breathing. Between March 2012 and August 2013 alone, at least 19 young people died as a result of taking NBOMe.[5] NBOMe is not always sold as LSD. It can also be sold under nicknames, such as smiles or N-bomb.

ARIA'S STORY

Thirteen-year-old Aria Doherty was a straight A student. Her hobbies ranged from art, writing, and acting to ice skating, fencing, and rock climbing. According to her family, Aria "made those around her feel loved and valued. . . . She was known for her kind, sensitive, funny personality and for being a fiercely loyal and protective friend."[6] As she grew up, Aria's parents had talked to her about the dangers of drug and alcohol abuse. They kept all prescription medications in a locked box and removed all alcohol from the home. They had no dangerous weapons in the house. But they weren't aware that another danger lurked in their cupboards: compressed air, used for cleaning computer keyboards.

On March 18, 2013, Aria was home alone when she decided to try something new—huffing, or inhaling a chemical substance. She took a can of compressed air to her bedroom, placed a piece of tape over her nostrils, and pressed the compressed air to her mouth. Aria's first time huffing was also

Cans of compressed air are great for cleaning electronics, but they can be deadly when misused.

her last. The chemicals she inhaled caused Aria to go into cardiac arrest. Her sister found her dead about an hour later with the can of compressed air still pressed against her face.

THE HIGH COST OF CLUB DRUGS

Derek, Alyssa, Roxanne, Arthur, Montana, and Aria were among the thousands of young people who abuse club drugs. Club drugs are drugs that people often take when they are at clubs, parties, or festivals or just hanging out with friends. They may take these drugs in hopes of improving their social experience or increasing their fun. Some people take club drugs on their own at home, as well. The most common club drugs include MDMA, LSD and other hallucinogens, ketamine, gamma-hydroxybutyrate (GHB), and Rohypnol. Inhalants are nondrug substances that are inhaled, often alone or with a small group of friends.

Abuse of club drugs is illegal. It is also dangerous. Club drugs can have side effects that cause serious illness or death. They can lead people to act in ways

USING MULTIPLE DRUGS

Most people who use club drugs also use alcohol, marijuana, methamphetamine, or other drugs, often at the same time. Some people take LSD and MDMA at the same time. Drug users have given this practice the name candy flipping. They call taking MDMA and psilocybin, or hallucinogenic mushrooms, at the same time hippie flipping. Bumping up means taking MDMA with cocaine. Using more than one substance at a time increases the danger, as drugs often interact with or increase the effects of other drugs.

The DEA sometimes uses drug detection dogs to find illegal substances being brought into the United States through airports.

they wouldn't normally act, making it easier for others to take advantage of them or hurt them. Club drugs can also cause dependence and addiction.

Oftentimes, the drugs people buy at parties or festivals are not what those selling them say they are. People taking these drugs cannot be 100 percent sure of what they are putting into their bodies. Because these drugs are illegal, they are not regulated or inspected for quality. Even if a person receives the drug he or she expects, there is no telling how strong the dose is. Some doses are weaker, while others are stronger. This can lead to unexpected—and even deadly—consequences. According to US Drug Enforcement Administration (DEA) spokesperson Joseph Moses, "Kids are being used as guinea pigs. The manufacturer didn't go through clinical trials, the person who orders and repackages it doesn't know what it's gonna do to somebody, and the user didn't know what it was going to do to them."[7]

CHAPTER TWO

CLUB DRUG HISTORY AND USE

Indigenous peoples of North America and South America have used natural substances to alter their state of mind for more than 10,000 years. The Aztecs of Mexico ingested mushrooms that caused hallucinations as part of their religious ceremonies. They believed eating the mushrooms helped them communicate with their gods. In North America, some Native Americans used peyote, a species of cactus, for its ability to cause hallucinations. By the late 1800s, some scientists had grown interested in the plant's effects. They were able to isolate the active substance in peyote, known as mescaline.

A man performs a traditional Aztec dance in Mexico.

▶

CREATING NEW DRUGS

Later, people sought to repeat the experience produced by peyote and psilocybin from mushrooms through manufactured drugs, including LSD and MDMA, both of which were produced as researchers looked for new ways to treat diseases. In 1938, Swiss chemist Albert Hofmann was trying to create new medicines from plants and fungi. He wanted to develop a medicine that would improve the function of the respiratory and circulatory systems. Among the substances he studied was ergot, a fungus that affects the rye plant. In its natural form, ergot is

Albert Hofmann headed the research department of the Swiss chemical company Sandoz.

deadly. Its accidental ingestion had killed hundreds of thousands of people over the years. But when used in small doses, compounds extracted from ergot could help to stop bleeding. Hofmann and other researchers discovered the chemical base of the ergot compounds, which they termed lysergic acid. In

Native Americans may have used up to 60 plant-derived drugs as part of their spiritual practices.[3]

his research, Hofmann then combined lysergic acid with other molecules in an attempt to create new substances that could prove medically useful. Among the substances he produced was lysergic acid diethylamide, or LSD.

The new substance was tested on animals but did not produce the desired effects of improving circulation and breathing. Instead, it seemed only to make the animals excited. Hofmann noted that the new substance "aroused no special interest. . . . Testing was therefore discontinued."[1]

But five years later, Hofmann returned to his LSD research because he said he had "a peculiar presentiment—the feeling that this substance could possess properties other than those established in the first investigations."[2] On April 16, 1943, Hofmann was synthesizing the compound when he started feeling weird sensations. He stopped his work and went home to rest. He felt restless and slightly dizzy. He laid down and entered what he later described as a "dream-like state" in which he "perceived an uninterrupted stream of fantastic pictures, extraordinary shapes with intense, kaleidoscopic play of colors."[4]

Hofmann was not sure what had happened, but he guessed LSD had touched his skin. He decided to experiment with the drug on himself to see if that were the case. He mixed a small amount of LSD in water and drank it. He started to feel dizzy and anxious. He had difficulty seeing clearly, experienced symptoms of paralysis, and felt a strange desire to laugh. The experience intensified as Hofmann tried to ride his bike home. By the time he got home, he was hallucinating. At first, the hallucinations were scary. As time passed, the scary hallucinations stopped and were replaced by vivid, colorful imagery that Hofmann found more pleasant. Several hours later, the effects of the drug started to fade. Hofmann had discovered that LSD had psychoactive properties. That is, it could affect the brain.

Hofmann's discovery led to further research. The Sandoz Company, for which Hofmann worked, distributed LSD for free to

"Everything in the room spun around, and the familiar objects and pieces of furniture assumed grotesque, threatening forms. They were in continuous motion, animated, as if driven by an inner relentlessness. The lady next door . . . was no longer Mrs. R, but rather a malevolent, insidious witch with a colored mask. . . . A demon had invaded me, had taken possession of my body, mind, and soul. . . . I was seized by the dreadful fear of going insane. I was taken to another world, another place, another time. My body seemed to be without sensation, lifeless, strange. Was I dying?"[5]

—Albert Hofmann, account of self-experiment with LSD, 1943

researchers. Throughout the late 1940s and 1950s, psychiatrists experimented with LSD in patient therapy. But they discovered no medical use for the drug. Even so, some psychiatrists, such as Timothy Leary, promoted use of the drug to young people as a way to "turn on, tune in, and drop out."[6] During the 1960s, as young people experimented widely with drugs, LSD became the drug of choice for many.

MORE NEW DRUGS

Research into MDMA began even earlier than LSD, but the drug did not become popular until the 1980s. In 1912, a German pharmaceutical company was working to develop a new drug to control bleeding. One of the chemical substances created during the process was MDMA. Because MDMA was further processed to create the desired drug, rather than used on its own, MDMA itself was largely ignored until the 1950s and 1960s, when some scientists began to study its effects on animals and humans.

In 1978, chemist Alexander Shulgin published a paper about the use of MDMA in people. He noted that the drug seemed to create feelings of trust and cause even quiet people to become talkative and open up to others. Shulgin recommended the drug be used to open communication between psychiatrists and their patients. The reputation of MDMA spread. It became so popular that about 30,000 doses were given monthly by psychiatrists and psychologists.[7]

Alexander Shulgin advocated for the use of MDMA and went on thousands of psychedelic trips with his wife, Ann.

As the medical use of MDMA grew, so did its recreational use. In the 1970s and 1980s, young people taking part in the New Age movement—who sought to create a new age of love through personal transformation—believed MDMA could produce mystical experiences. In the 1980s, MDMA also reached a new crowd—those who attended secret dance parties called raves. Raves first gained popularity in Europe but soon spread to the United States and other parts of the world.

As raves spread, the number of drugs used at them increased. By the 1990s, GHB, ketamine, and Rohypnol had appeared on the rave scene. GHB had first been synthesized in 1960 by a researcher trying to create an anesthetic. Although the drug made users unconscious quickly, as desired, it did not block pain signals, so it was not useful as an anesthetic. However, some people took it to help them sleep at home. Others used the drug because it was believed to help build muscle mass. Many enjoyed the dreamlike state produced by the drug and began to use it at raves and dance clubs.

Ketamine, first synthesized in 1962, was also originally intended as an anesthetic. But its ability to produce hallucinations led some people to abuse it as a club drug.

Developed in 1975, the sedative Rohypnol was approved for use in several European

PROJECT MK-ULTRA

In the 1950s and 1960s, the Central Intelligence Agency (CIA) conducted a secret program called MK-Ultra. In the program, the CIA experimented with LSD, MDMA, and other substances on volunteers and unknowing subjects. The purpose was to develop psychological weapons that could be used to control behavior or leave large groups of people incapacitated for long periods of time. Although MDMA was quickly dismissed as useless for this purpose, researchers thought LSD showed some promise. According to one report, the drug "is capable of rendering whole groups of people, including military forces, indifferent to their surroundings and situations, interfering with planning and judgment, and even creating apprehension, uncontrollable confusion, and terror."[8] The experiments ended in the early 1970s. The program was discovered by New York Times reporter Seymour Hersh, who published a story about it in 1974. As a result, President Gerald Ford prohibited drug experimentation on anyone who had not given his or her consent in writing.

countries but not in the United States. Abuse of the drug began almost as soon as it was first manufactured. In some cases, people would secretly put it into others' drinks at clubs or parties. The drug placed the people who took it into a nearly comatose state, making it easy for the attackers to sexually assault or rob them.

CLUB DRUGS AND THE LAW

In 1970, the US government passed the Controlled Substances Act (CSA). This act placed drugs into five schedules, or categories, based on their legitimate medical uses and their potential for abuse and addiction. The CSA continues to govern drug use today.

Schedule I drugs have no medical value and are highly addictive. They include club drugs such as LSD, MDMA, psilocybin, and GHB. Marijuana and heroin are also Schedule I drugs.

Schedule II drugs have medical value but are highly addictive and have high potential for abuse. Prescription painkillers such as oxycodone and hydromorphone fall into this category, as does methamphetamine. Schedule III drugs have medical value and have a low to moderate risk of addiction. Ketamine is an example of a Schedule III drug. Schedule IV and Schedule V drugs also have medical value. The potential for addiction and abuse of these drugs is low. Examples of Schedule IV drugs include Xanax and Valium. Cough medicine with codeine is an example of a Schedule V drug.

WHO USES CLUB DRUGS

Although club drugs are illegal, many people continue to use them. The National Survey on Drug Use and Health (NSDUH) is conducted by the US government's Substance Abuse and Mental Health Services Administration (SAMHSA) every year. In 2015, the survey revealed that about 4.7 million people over the age of 12 used hallucinogens at least once during the year.[9] For the purposes of the survey, most club drugs were included in the category of hallucinogens, including LSD, psilocybin, peyote, ecstasy, and ketamine.

About 1 percent of 12th grade students reported using the club drugs ketamine, GHB, and Rohypnol at least once in 2016.[10]

Monitoring the Future, a national survey sponsored by the National Institute on Drug Abuse (NIDA), further breaks down

MOST USED DRUGS AT US RAVES AND MUSIC FESTIVALS[12]

PRODUCT	PERCENT REPORTING USE OF SUBSTANCE
ALCOHOL	97.1%
MARIJUANA	88.4%
ENERGY DRINKS	66.3%
TOBACCO	62.4%
MDMA	60.9%
LSD	44.3%
PSILOCYBIN	40.7%
COCAINE	34.2%
AMPHETAMINE	27.0%
NITROUS OXIDE	20.7%
KETAMINE	15.4%
CAFFEINE TABLETS	11.5%

The 2013 Global Drug Survey asked more than 22,000 drug users about their substance use habits at raves and music festivals.

the use of specific drugs among young people in grades 8, 10, and 12. In 2016, 1.2 percent of eighth graders, 3.2 percent of tenth graders, and 4.9 percent of twelfth graders reported they had used LSD at least once in their lives. This marked a dramatic decrease in LSD use from 20 years earlier, when 5.1 percent of eighth graders, 9.4 percent of tenth graders, and 12.6 percent of twelfth graders reported using LSD at some point in their lives.[11]

Monitoring the Future also surveys how many people are currently using a drug. Current use is defined as having used the drug in the 30 days before taking the survey. According to the survey's results, only 0.4 percent of eighth graders, 0.7 percent of tenth graders, and 1 percent of twelfth graders were current LSD users.[13]

According to the NSDUH, in 2015, an estimated 2.6 million people over the age of 12 used MDMA at least once during the year. More than 18 million people had tried it during their lifetimes.[14] The 2016 Monitoring the Future survey showed that 1.7 percent of eighth grade students, 2.8 percent of tenth grade students, and 4.9 percent of twelfth grade students had tried MDMA at least once in their lives. Less than 1 percent of students in all three monitored grades reported using MDMA in the 30 days before the survey.[15]

Inhalant users tend to be younger than users of other club drugs. This may be because younger kids who wish to experiment with drugs may not be able to easily obtain other drugs. However, it is easy to find household items that can be inhaled. Another possible reason is younger kids do not understand the dangers of inhalants. Monitoring the Future researchers asked students whether they thought use of a specific drug was risky. About 60 percent of eighth and tenth graders did not feel there was a great risk in trying inhalants once or twice. In 2016, 7.7 percent of eighth graders, 6.6 percent of tenth graders, and 5 percent of twelfth graders admitted to trying inhalants at least once in their lives.[16]

CHAPTER THREE

LSD

LSD is a type of drug known as a hallucinogen. Hallucinogens are drugs that can cause hallucinations. A hallucination involves seeing, hearing, smelling, feeling, and even tasting things that are not present. LSD goes by many nicknames, including acid, blotter, California sunshine, dots, and electric Kool-Aid.

People use various words to describe the experiences they have when they use drugs or alcohol. When people drink too much alcohol, they say they get buzzed or drunk. When they use marijuana, people say they get high. When people take hallucinogens, such as LSD, they are taking a trip.

HOW LSD IS MADE AND TAKEN

The process of manufacturing LSD is complex and dangerous. It requires use of the toxic fungus ergot. Lysergic acid is extracted

A square of LSD blotting paper is about the size of a postage stamp. People taking the drug place the paper on their tongues.

from the ergot using a host of toxic, flammable, and explosive chemicals. Once the LSD has been produced and purified, it is crystallized into a colorless, odorless powder that may taste slightly bitter. The powder may be pressed into tiny tablets known as microdots. Or, it can be dissolved in water or added to a sugar cube or gelatin square.

But the most common way to take LSD today is on blotting paper. Blotting paper is a sheet of cotton that absorbs liquid. The blotting paper used for LSD is often printed with colorful cartoons or other graphics. It is dipped into a solution of LSD dissolved in alcohol. The blotting paper is allowed to dry and then perforated into quarter-inch (0.64 cm) squares. Each square contains one dose of LSD. A single sheet of blotting paper might contain up to 100 doses. The precise strength of that dose depends on the strength of the LSD solution that was used. To take the drug, the user chews

Almost all illicit LSD in the United States is believed to be produced by fewer than a dozen labs in northern California.

and swallows a square of blotting paper. Some people also place the blotting paper under an eyelid and allow the drug to be absorbed through the mucus membrane there.

LSD is the most powerful psychoactive substance known to science. The doses of many common drugs are measured in milligrams. For instance, an over-the-counter pill of ibuprofen might be 200 milligrams. LSD is such a powerful substance that it is measured in micrograms. There are 1,000 micrograms in 1 milligram. A dose as small as 25 micrograms—about the weight of two grains of salt—of LSD can produce effects on the user. Today, the most common LSD dose is around 100 micrograms.

EFFECTS OF LSD

The effects of LSD are not immediate but usually begin within 30 to 60 minutes of taking the drug. Physical effects of LSD can include enlarged pupils, raised body temperature, increased heart rate and blood pressure, sweating, loss of appetite, tremors, and sleeplessness.

Just 2 pounds (0.9 kg) of LSD would be enough to affect the entire population of New York City for several hours.[1]

Only about 0.1 percent of the LSD in a dose reaches the brain, and it remains there for only 15 minutes or so before being broken down. But the effects of the drug last much longer. Scientists believe that LSD works by attaching to receptors on the brain's neurons, or nerve cells. Receptors are structures or molecules on a neuron that recognize and attach to specific chemicals called neurotransmitters. Neurotransmitters help send messages to brain cells to create responses in the body. Researchers believe LSD specifically attaches to receptors meant to recognize serotonin, a neurotransmitter connected to mood, appetite, and sensory perception. LSD may cause the serotonin receptors to increase the activation of sensory neurons, leading to hallucinations and altered senses. People using the drug

LSD can affect how users see the world.

may think the objects around them have come to life. Colors might appear richer and sounds seem clearer. Some people may experience synesthesia, in which the senses get mixed, leading a person to see music or hear colors, for example. Users may lose track of time and even of their own bodies, feeling as if they have become part of the universe. Some people experience feelings of happiness, in which everything seems magical and beautiful.

But the effects of LSD are unpredictable. No two experiences will be the same. Some people using LSD see or hear things that are frightening. Others see or hear things that are enjoyable. Even the same person may experience a pleasurable trip one time and a frightening one the next time. During bad trips, people can experience terrifying thoughts, fear of death or losing control, and panic attacks.

How long someone experiences the effects of LSD depends on the dose taken. If a dose of 100 micrograms is taken, an experience can last about six to eight hours. High doses can lead to longer and more intense experiences.

LONG-TERM EFFECTS

An LSD overdose may result in psychological distress but usually does not cause severe physical harm. A person who has overdosed on LSD may experience fear and anxiety that does not end until the trip is over. Individuals who use LSD often report feeling exhausted the next day as well.

Although LSD alone rarely causes death, people have been injured and even died as a result of their behaviors while experiencing a trip. For example, people using LSD may attempt to jump off buildings because they think they can fly. Or they

NEVER AGAIN

One person who used LSD on two occasions at the age of 18 later described her experiences to researchers. The first time, she had enjoyed the trip. The second time started out pleasurably as well. She saw colorful laser beams shooting out of her dog's tail and exploding on the ceiling, but she wasn't afraid because she knew it wasn't real. But hours later, her heart was pounding, and her joints ached. She continued to hallucinate. After eating some candy, she thought her blood had turned to chocolate. She worried that someone would see her as a big piece of candy and wrap her up. When she looked in the mirror, she saw her skin melt away to reveal her skull. After 12 hours, the user was still experiencing her trip. She feared she would have to kill herself to make it stop. Finally, after 30 hours, the trip ended. But it took the user two weeks to feel normal again. She promised herself she would never use LSD again.

might step into traffic, thinking they have the superhuman ability to stop a truck. A number of people using LSD have also committed suicide.

LSD does not cause addiction. The body quickly builds up a tolerance to the drug, meaning that if someone takes LSD several days in a row, he or she will feel no effects by the third or fourth day. After a person stops taking the drug for a few days, the tolerance disappears. The body does not experience withdrawal symptoms when the drug is not taken regularly.

Although LSD causes few physical long-term effects, it can cause long-term psychological issues. The drug can cause depression or worsen mental illnesses such as schizophrenia. In rare cases, LSD use can lead to psychosis. Some long-term LSD users have difficulty sleeping and lose interest in eating and taking care of themselves. They may stop participating in the real world.

Some users have flashbacks, or brief periods during which they re-experience some aspect

THE IMPORTANCE OF PLACE

According to some LSD users, the set and setting of an LSD trip play important parts in whether a person will have a good or bad trip. Set refers to the person's mind-set when taking the LSD. A person who is calm and relaxed before taking the drug is believed to be more likely to have a positive experience. Someone feeling nervous or reluctant might have a bad trip. Setting refers to the user's physical surroundings. A relaxing and pleasant setting is thought to produce a more pleasurable experience, while a busy location with many strangers may lead to a scary trip.

People with schizophrenia may experience hallucinations and struggle with their emotions. Taking LSD can make the symptoms of schizophrenia worse.

of a previous trip, such as altered images. Flashbacks usually last only a few seconds. They can occur weeks or even months after a person last used LSD. They may be triggered by stress, fatigue, or use of other drugs.

POTENTIAL MEDICAL USES OF LSD

The Multidisciplinary Association for Psychedelic Studies (MAPS) is a large, nonprofit organization headquartered in Santa Cruz,

California, that promotes research on hallucinogens. MAPS funds research, including government-approved clinical trials, on drugs such as LSD. MAPS has contributed to research in Switzerland that examined LSD-assisted therapy for treating anxiety in people with life-threatening diseases. It found that using two doses of LSD, spaced three weeks apart, during therapy sessions produced lasting reductions in anxiety.

Research has also shown that LSD may help treat migraines and cluster headaches—intense headaches that occur around one eye and that can last weeks or months. In addition, there is some evidence that LSD may have pain-relieving properties, although more research is needed. The biggest obstacle to using LSD as a pain reliever is finding a dose that can relieve pain without causing hours-long hallucinations.

MICRO-DOSING

Micro-dosing LSD involves taking about 10 micrograms of LSD every couple of days. This is not meant to produce hallucinations. Instead, users believe micro-doses improve their moods and energy levels. The goal is to help increase creativity and energy in order to get the best results at work. Today, micro-dosing is especially popular in California's Silicon Valley. The area is home to start-up and high-tech companies that always need to produce new products and services. Micro-dosing LSD is seen by some as a way to maintain a competitive edge. Little research has been done on the possible negative health and psychological effects of micro-dosing.

OTHER HALLUCINOGENS

Many substances other than LSD have hallucinogenic properties. Several of these, including psilocybin, peyote, and N,N-dimethyltryptamine (DMT), occur naturally.

Psilocybin is found in several species of mushrooms grown in North and South America. These mushrooms are often referred to as magic mushrooms or shrooms. Some people harvest mushrooms from the wild. Others grow the mushrooms at home or purchase them from friends.

Hallucinogenic mushrooms contain psilocin in addition to psilocybin. Psilocin is present only in trace amounts but is more potent than psilocybin. The most

A licensed dealer in Texas handles the peyote buttons he harvested.

potent mushrooms contain about 2 percent psilocybin. Since the majority of a mushroom is water, hallucinogenic mushrooms are usually dried before they are eaten. This increases the concentration of psilocybin in the mushroom. When the mushroom is eaten, the liver converts psilocybin into psilocin, which enters the bloodstream and reaches the brain.

Users generally eat two to four dried mushrooms to experience hallucinogenic effects. If users chew the mushrooms well and hold them in their mouth, they may begin to experience effects within seven or eight minutes. Those who swallow the mushrooms quickly may not experience an effect for 30 to 45 minutes. Some people brew the dried mushrooms in a tea or mix them with other foods to mask their bitter flavor. Psilocybin can also be refined into a crystallized white powder.

EATING WILD MUSHROOMS

Harvesting wild mushrooms in hopes of taking a psilocybin trip can be dangerous. It's easy to mistake poisonous mushrooms for ones containing psilocybin. Some wild mushrooms, including the death cap, can cause vomiting, diarrhea, and dehydration. They may also seriously damage the liver, leading the patient to need a transplant.

The effects of psilocybin are similar to those of LSD, although psilocybin is much less potent. Low doses of psilocybin cause people to relax. They may make the user yawn or feel restless. Within an hour or two, the user may experience heightened visual perception. For example, colors may seem brighter. The user may also feel

Hallucinogenic mushrooms can affect people in different ways, and it can be hard to distinguish various kinds of mushrooms.

an uncontrollable urge to laugh. Increasing the dose may cause hallucinations, difficulty thinking, and changes in mood. It also can have physical effects such as light-headedness; numbness of the tongue, lips, or mouth; shivering or sweating; and nausea. Some people feel as if they are separating from their bodies. Some people have reported experiencing paranoia or panic attacks during a psilocybin trip. A trip can last between two and six hours, depending on the dose taken.

It appears to be extremely difficult to overdose and die from psilocybin. It is not a toxic substance. One study estimated that an individual would need to consume nearly 38 pounds (17 kg) of fresh psilocybin at one time to cause death.[1] However, people are more likely to be injured or die from accidents while under the influence of psilocybin.

PEYOTE

Peyote is a cactus that grows in the southwestern United States and northwestern Mexico. It contains the hallucinogen mescaline. Small, disc-shaped lumps at the top of the plant are known as peyote buttons. These buttons can be eaten fresh or dried and then swallowed without chewing. Peyote can also be smoked with tobacco or marijuana, processed into a powder, or brewed in tea. A single dose of peyote may include 4 to 12 buttons.

Peyote's chemical structure is unlike that of LSD or psilocybin. Instead, it is more similar to the structure of amphetamines, stimulant drugs that increase energy and suppress appetite. Like amphetamines, peyote causes increased heart rate and blood pressure as well as enlarged pupils. It can also cause nausea, vomiting, headaches, dizziness, sweating, and stomach cramps. These symptoms can last up to 3 hours. After the physical symptoms subside, the user experiences hallucinogenic

The peyote cactus can live up to 100 years, with buttons repeatedly harvested from it.

effects similar to those caused by LSD. The user may also feel a deep sense of spiritual understanding or connection. A peyote trip can last up to 12 hours. Some users experience fatigue, anxiety, or depression after taking peyote.

Little research has been done on the long-term effects of peyote use. A study on Native American peyote users did not find any lasting psychological or intellectual effects from regular peyote use. Peyote overdose is nearly impossible because, in high quantities, the drug causes vomiting. However, high doses can cause panic attacks.

DMT

DMT occurs naturally in many trees, vines, grasses, and mushrooms, as well as in some species of toads, moth larvae, grubs, and fish. It can also be synthetically manufactured. DMT is usually snorted, smoked, or injected. In South America, it is sometimes brewed into a tea known as ayahuasca.

THE PEYOTE ROAD

Although peyote is a Schedule I drug, members of the Native American Church are legally allowed to use it as part of their religious rituals. Founded in 1918, the Native American Church combines Christian and Native American beliefs. Members follow a set of teachings known as the Peyote Road. The Peyote Road stresses the importance of brotherly love, care for family, self-reliance, and avoidance of alcohol.

Members see eating peyote as a way to communicate with God. Today, the Native American Church has about 300,000 members.[3]

Peyote grows wild near Texas's border with Mexico.

Unlike those of other hallucinogens, the effects of DMT are felt quickly and are short lived, ending after only 15 to 30 minutes. DMT causes intense, often frightening hallucinations, an altered sense of time, and a distorted body image. Physical effects include increased blood pressure and heart rate, dizziness, enlarged pupils, involuntary eye movements, lack of muscle coordination, and even seizures. At high doses, DMT can cause a user to fall into a coma or stop breathing.

POTENTIAL MEDICAL USES OF HALLUCINOGENS

Researchers have studied the possibility of using naturally occurring hallucinogens for medical purposes. There is evidence that psilocybin can reduce anxiety and depression, with results lasting months. Psilocybin has also been shown to help people dealing with obsessive-compulsive disorder. It has helped with cluster headaches and migraines, too. In some cases, psilocybin has helped reduce smoking and drinking in users.

Peyote has long been used as a folk remedy in Mexico. People use it to treat arthritis, tuberculosis, influenza, diabetes, and even snake and scorpion bites. Among some Native American groups, peyote is also used to treat alcohol and drug abuse and addiction, with some success. According to Dr. Karl A. Menninger, "Peyote is not harmful. . . . It is a better antidote to alcohol than anything [the] American Medical Association and the public health services have come up with."[4]

AYAHUASCA RETREATS

Many indigenous peoples of South America use ayahuasca in traditional ceremonies for healing and spiritual growth. Today, ayahuasca fuels a small tourist industry. People from other parts of the world travel to locations in Peru, Brazil, and other parts of South America where ayahuasca is legal. There, they participate in retreats that center on ayahuasca rituals. Places such as the Rainforest Healing Center in Iquitos, Peru, and the Nimea Kaya Healing Center in Pucallpa, Peru, offer visitors the opportunity to use ayahuasca. Websites have even sprung up providing reviews of the retreats, so tourists can make more informed decisions.

MDMA

MDMA is a synthetic drug with similarities to hallucinogens and amphetamines. Scientists also classify MDMA as an empathogen or entactogen. These drugs make people willing to open up about their feelings and feel more connected to other people.

MDMA in tablet form is commonly known as ecstasy. It is also called Adam, Clarity, Eve, Lover's Speed, Peace, Uppers, Rolls, Beans, X, and XTC. Molly is a powdered form of MDMA that many users believe contains pure MDMA, but both ecstasy tablets and Molly powder often contain other harmful substances.

MDMA PRODUCTION

Because MDMA is illegal, most of the world's supply of the drug is manufactured in illicit labs. Although MDMA is relatively easy to manufacture, it requires specialized ingredients, many of which

Drug dealers sell their product to teens at raves and other parties.

are toxic. One of the needed ingredients is safrole, an oil found in the fruit and bark of the sassafras plant. Safrole oil is a precursor chemical in the production of MDMA. That means it is used to make another type of chemical. The safrole oil must be combined with numerous other chemicals to produce MDMA.

MDMA costs less than two cents per tablet to manufacture.

The resulting chemical is crystallized into a fine white powder. The powder may then be colored and pressed into pills, often featuring cartoon images. Ecstasy pills can be made to look like anything. In the summer of 2017, police in Germany seized about 5,000 ecstasy pills shaped like President Donald Trump's head. In June 2017, police in Las Vegas, Nevada, seized thousands of ecstasy pills in the shape of blue Transformers. Each ecstasy pill may contain 50 to 150 milligrams of MDMA. When sold as Molly, MDMA often remains in powder form. The powder may be snorted, dissolved in water, or placed in a capsule and swallowed.

MDMA = ECSTASY = MOLLY

According to a study conducted by Joseph Palamar, a professor of population health at New York University, many young drug users do not realize that MDMA, ecstasy, and Molly are all the same drug. When asked if they use ecstasy, young people may say no, even though they use Molly. According to Palamar, "We have this young generation who maybe have heard of ecstasy from friends or in health class, then this 'new' drug called Molly comes around and they don't know that it's ecstasy. That's a major issue."[1]

ECSTASY EFFECTS

Users often start with one
ecstasy pill and then take
another as the effects begin to wear off. The effects of MDMA
kick in about 45 minutes after taking the drug. MDMA works
by releasing serotonin in the brain. Since serotonin sends
messages influencing mood, people often feel good when they
take MDMA. They may feel more extroverted, or outgoing and
talkative, as well as more empathetic and emotionally open.
People who take MDMA also report lower levels of aggression.
Some people notice their senses
are enhanced, much as occurs
with hallucinogens.

MDMA can have several
side effects, including nausea,
vomiting, increased blood
pressure, and faintness. Other
side effects can include
confusion, anxiety, tremors, rapid
eye movement, jaw clenching,
teeth grinding, sweating,
dehydration, lack of appetite,
restless legs, headache, and
muscle soreness.

Production of 2.2 pounds (1 kg) of MDMA results in 13 to 22 pounds (6 to 10 kg) of toxic waste.[2]

LIST 1 CHEMICALS

Safrole oil is highly regulated in the United States and is classified as a List I Chemical by the DEA. This means it is a chemical used to make illegal drugs. The DEA watches companies that import and sell safrole oil. The companies have to track everything they do with it—who they buy it from, how much money was spent, and what quantity was purchased. The same records have to be kept when selling safrole to other companies.

In some cases, especially when taken in a warm environment or while participating in physical activity, MDMA can be deadly. The drug can increase body temperature to unsafe levels, known as hyperthermia. Doctors have noted cases in which body temperatures reached as high as 109 degrees Fahrenheit (43°C).[3] Such elevated body temperatures can cause organs to shut down, leading to death. According to Dr. Marc Futernick of Dignity Health California Hospital Medical Center, "There's no

The number of emergency department visits in the United States in which the patient reported use of MDMA more than doubled between 2004 and 2011.[4]

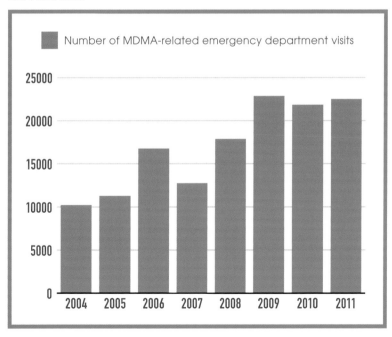

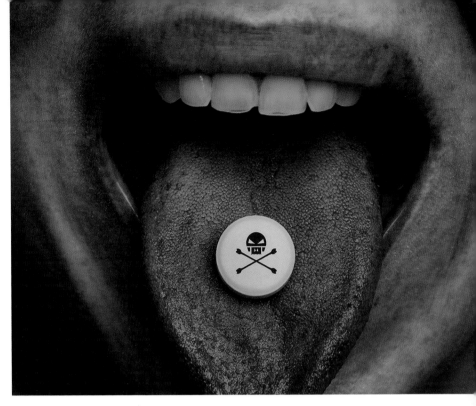

MDMA pills often feature logos, cartoons, or icons.

other way to describe it other than it will melt your organs and do damage to your organs to the point you will die."[5] Death can also occur if users who have become overheated drink too much water, causing an imbalance in the body's sodium levels that can lead to fatal seizures. MDMA can also cause kidney failure or swelling of the brain, both of which can kill users.

TOO TRUSTING

Because MDMA enhances feelings of empathy and trust, people using the drug may be more likely to trust someone they've just met. These trusting feelings may lead a user to go along with anything someone else suggests. The release of serotonin also triggers hormones that increase feelings of attraction,

Predators can use MDMA to prey on people whose judgment is clouded by the drug.

love, and sexual arousal. This may lead users to make decisions about relationships that they wouldn't make when not using the drug, including having sex with strangers. According to Dr. Ian Hindmarch, a professor at the University of Surrey in Australia, "MDMA might make victims feel loved up, and so more liable

to 'consent' to sex."[6] In other words, the person may say yes to a situation he or she would normally say no to. According to some legal experts, a person who knowingly takes advantage of someone using MDMA may be guilty of sexual assault.

In addition, being too open and trusting can make users vulnerable to being manipulated or taken advantage of. According to psychologist Kathryn Stamoulis, MDMA's "purpose is to create a feeling of bonding, euphoria [overwhelming happiness], relaxation, etc., so a person is not able to accurately judge a situation's risk of threat."[7]

LONG-TERM EFFECTS

The effects of MDMA generally wear off after about three hours. But users may continue to experience side effects for several days. Since MDMA uses up the body's stores of serotonin, which helps regulate mood, the body needs time to replenish its supply. Until serotonin is built up again, people feel down and cranky. Some users also experience muscle aches, chills, abdominal pain, tremors, and suicidal feelings. In addition, MDMA use can cause sleep and memory problems. There's conflicting evidence on whether long-term heavy MDMA use causes permanent damage to the serotonin receptors in the brain.

"I hear a lot of people talking about ecstasy, calling it a fun, harmless drug. All I can think is: If they only knew. In five months, I went from living somewhat responsibly, while pursuing my dream, to be a person who didn't care about a thing. And the higher I got, the deeper I sank into a dark, lonely place. When I did sleep, I had nightmares and the shakes. I had pasty skin, a throbbing head, and the beginnings of feeling paranoid. . . . Ecstasy took my strength, my motivation, my dreams, my friends, my apartment, my money, and most of all, my sanity."[8]

—Lynn, ecstasy user

MDMA users can also develop tolerance to the drug. This means that, over time, they need to take higher doses to get the same effect. According to one user, "The more you do it the less good you feel while on it and the worse you feel coming down."[9] Scientists are not yet sure whether people can become addicted to MDMA, but some users report experiencing cravings for the drug and continuing to use it despite negative consequences, both signs of addiction.

AN IMPURE DRUG

Because MDMA is illegal and is produced in secret laboratories, it is almost impossible to know what drugs sold as MDMA actually contain. Ecstasy pills often contain a mix of MDMA and amphetamines, caffeine, the cough medicine dextromethorphan (DXM), the diet drug ephedrine, heroin, or cocaine. In many cases, these drugs are even more dangerous than MDMA and can cause severe side effects when mixed.

In addition, there is no way to regulate the dose of MDMA in an ecstasy pill. In some cases, pills sold as ecstasy contain no MDMA at all. Although some people believe that Molly is pure MDMA, in many cases it contains no MDMA either. Instead, it may contain synthetic cathinones, otherwise known as bath salts. These drugs can cause effects similar to MDMA, including lowered inhibitions, increased energy, and agitation. Other effects can include hallucinations, paranoia, and panic attacks.

Physical effects include increased heart rate and blood pressure, nosebleeds, sweating, and nausea. In some cases, bath salts have caused death.

POTENTIAL MEDICAL USES OF MDMA

In November 2017, the FDA approved clinical trials on the use of MDMA for post-traumatic stress disorder (PTSD). Previous research indicates that MDMA can reduce the fear that occurs with traumatic memories when used in combination with therapy. Because it also makes people more socially open, it helps strengthen the relationship between patients and counselors. In one study, about 85 percent of the people who used MDMA with therapy to treat PTSD were free of symptoms four years later.[10]

In addition, in 2017, researchers in London began a study to determine whether MDMA could help treat people addicted to alcohol. Other London researchers are investigating the potential for MDMA to aid in relationship counseling by creating an environment where couples feel free to be completely open with one another.

Bath salts may look like ordinary salt, but they can be deadly when ingested.

CHAPTER SIX

KETAMINE, GHB, AND ROHYPNOL

Other drugs commonly used at clubs and festivals include ketamine, GHB, and Rohypnol. All three slow the activity of the central nervous system.

Ketamine was first developed as an anesthetic. Like other anesthetics used for surgery, it causes people to fall asleep, stops them from feeling pain, and prevents them from remembering the experience. Unlike other anesthetics, ketamine does not have an impact on breathing or heart rate, making it safe to use, especially in children.

But ketamine can cause people to experience hallucinations when they wake up. For this reason, ketamine is no longer

Ketamine is often snorted as a powder, though it comes in other forms as well.

frequently used as an anesthetic for adults. Doctors do not want patients to wake up after surgery and not know what is happening because of hallucinations. A patient could be injured or hurt bystanders during such a reaction.

LIQUID, POWDER, PILL

According to the DEA, most illicit ketamine in the United States today enters the country through Mexico. Drug traffickers either make the ketamine in Mexico and bring it to the United States or smuggle supplies manufactured in other countries through Mexico and into the United States. Legal supplies of liquid ketamine are sometimes stolen. Manufacturers then evaporate the liquid to produce ketamine crystals, which they crush into a powder.

Ketamine can be manufactured as a colorless, odorless liquid or a white powder, crystal, tablet, or capsule. Powdered ketamine can be snorted or mixed with a liquid and drunk. Or it may be rolled with marijuana or tobacco and smoked. Ketamine tablets are swallowed, while liquid ketamine can be injected or drunk.

Similar to many other drugs, ketamine can be injected for a quick high.

When taken by mouth, ketamine can take 30 minutes to produce effects. A ketamine injection can take effect in as little as 30 seconds. Nicknames for ketamine include special K, vitamin K, liquid E, Kit Kat, k-hole, and cat valium.

KETAMINE EFFECTS

The same hallucinogenic effects that make ketamine a poor choice for anesthesia make it a desirable drug for recreational users. Ketamine blocks glutamate, a neurotransmitter responsible for communication between parts of the brain and the body. Low doses of ketamine create feelings similar to being drunk, including lack of coordination, lowered inhibitions, and a feeling of calm and relaxation. Users refer to a relatively mild experience on ketamine as going to k-land. At higher doses, users report a dissociative effect. That is, they feel they have left, or become dissociated from, their bodies. Users commonly refer to this as going down the k-hole.

The k-hole experience can be different for various people. Some have described it as floating or hovering or feeling as if light is going through their bodies. Others feel as if their bodies are weightless. The experience can also include hallucinations or visions, a feeling of connection with the universe, and near-death experiences. Some users are aware of what is happening around them but find it impossible to move.

Ketamine causes several side effects, including chest pains and increased heart rate and blood pressure. In addition, ketamine may cause inflammation of the bile ducts connecting the liver to the gallbladder, leading to

DXM USE AND ABUSE

DXM is a drug in many over-the-counter cough medicines. It does not have any psychoactive effects when taken at normal doses. However, when taken at high doses, it can cause effects similar to those produced by ketamine, including hallucinations or dissociation. The practice of taking DXM to get high is known as robo-tripping or skitting. DXM can cause an increase in blood pressure, stomach pains, lack of energy, and slurred speech. DXM abuse can lead to addiction.

severe stomach pain, known as K cramps. One user described the cramps as "possibly one of the most painful physical experiences a drug user will go through. Imagine a severely upset stomach that's ingested a bottle of bleach and then been set upon by a knife-wielding maniac."[1] A ketamine overdose can cause unconsciousness and potentially deadly breathing problems.

Although the hallucinogenic effects of ketamine wear off after about 90 minutes, the drug can continue to affect a person's judgment, coordination, and senses for up to 24 hours. In addition, higher doses of ketamine can cause long-term issues, including memory loss. People may not remember what happened while they were taking ketamine or the sensations they experienced while under its influence. People who have used ketamine have performed worse on tests of memory and brain function. One study found that frequent ketamine users had problems with memory function three days after they last used ketamine. Long-term use of ketamine has been linked to depression and delusions, or beliefs not based in reality. Some users experience flashbacks up to several weeks after using ketamine. Heavy ketamine users may also experience severe bladder and kidney damage.

MEDICAL USES OF KETAMINE

In addition to being used as an anesthetic, ketamine can be used as a pain reliever. Scientists are also researching its effectiveness in treating depression. Although results of some of these studies are promising, the effects of ketamine on depression appear to last only a few days or weeks.

In recent years, ketamine clinics have opened around the United States. The clinics provide infusion therapy, which involves giving ketamine through an intravenous (IV) injection to treat various conditions, including chronic pain, depression, PTSD, and migraines. Although these clinics are legal, some people have expressed concern that they are not adequately regulated. In addition, there are no agreed-upon guidelines for ketamine treatments. Although ketamine appears to be a relatively safe drug, the lack of guidelines may cause problems and confusion when trying to determine if the ketamine infusions are actually working.

Ketamine continues to be used as an anesthetic for animal surgeries. Veterinary clinics are sometimes robbed for their supplies of ketamine.

GHB

GHB is used as an anesthetic in Europe. It is illegal in the United States because of its potential for overdose and abuse. However, people suffering from the sleeping disorder narcolepsy can obtain GHB by prescription.

The drug's illegal status has not stopped people in the United States from making and selling GHB, which is relatively easy to manufacture. The process begins with the chemical

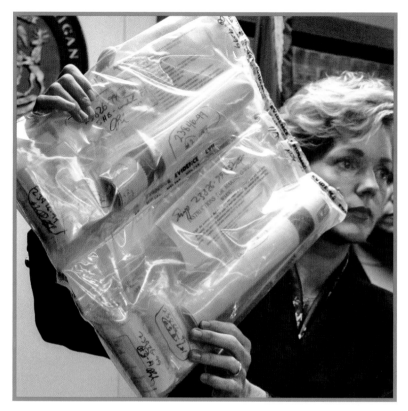

Authorities have arrested people who have made their own GHB from materials purchased on the internet.

gamma-butyrolactone (GBL), which is found in many products, from floor cleaners to nail polish. Illicit manufacturers combine GBL with chemicals found in laundry detergent, drain cleaners, and other easy-to-get household items. The chemical reaction between these substances produces GHB.

GHB can be sold as an odorless, colorless liquid or as a powder. The powder form is usually dissolved in water or juice and drunk. GHB is also sold by the names G, Georgia home boy, goop, grievous bodily harm, liquid ecstasy, liquid X, and scoop.

GHB EFFECTS

GHB occurs naturally in the brain and body but in much lower concentrations than a person receives when taking the drug. Scientists have found evidence that when users take GHB, it acts on receptors in the brain made to receive the neurotransmitter gamma-aminobutyric acid (GABA). GABA slows the brain's activity in preparation for sleep.

The effects of GHB become noticeable within 15 minutes of taking the drug and can last several hours. In small doses, GHB produces effects similar to those of alcohol and MDMA. Users feel relaxed, calm, and sociable. They may also experience memory lapses and forgetfulness. Physical effects include blurred vision, dizziness, and lack of coordination. At higher doses, users may experience memory loss, headache, light-headedness, slurred speech, and drowsiness.

The concentration of powdered GHB in a liquid can be difficult to determine, making

GHB FOR BODYBUILDING?

In the 1980s, GHB became popular as a health supplement. Bodybuilders used the drug to help build muscle mass and reduce body fat. Subsequent studies have shown that GHB doesn't increase muscle. But it does increase deep-wave sleep, the deep, dream-producing state of sleep. Scientists believe that the body produces most of its growth hormone during deep-wave sleep. So if a person is getting more deep-wave sleep, his or her body may produce more growth hormone, leading to bigger muscles. In recent years, GHB has seen renewed use among celebrities looking to lose weight or build muscle for upcoming roles.

it common for a person to take
more GHB than intended. The
difference between the dose
needed to create an effect and
the lethal dose is very small,
which means that overdose can occur easily. A GHB overdose can
make a person fall into a coma within 30 minutes of taking the
drug. Because GHB depresses the central nervous system, it can
cause a person's heart rate and breathing to slow or stop, leading
to death.

People who go into a GHB coma may suddenly recover and wake up, which is unusual for such a serious condition.

Few studies have examined the long-term effects of GHB use.
People who use the drug frequently may develop a tolerance,
needing more of the drug over time. If they stop using the drug,
they may experience withdrawal symptoms, including trouble
sleeping, anxiety, tremors, agitation, and elevated heart rate and
blood pressure.

ROHYPNOL

Rohypnol is the trade name for the drug flunitrazepam, which
may also be sold under other generic names. Although widely
used in Europe, Central America, and South America to treat
sleep disorders, anxiety, and alcohol withdrawal, Rohypnol has
never been approved for use in the United States.

Even so, the drug is frequently smuggled into the country
from Mexico and South America. It comes in caplet form.

Rohypnol caplets used to be white and dissolve into a clear powder in drinks. But after reports that the drug was being slipped into women's drinks by men who then sexually assaulted them, the manufacturer changed the drug's form. Rohypnol now comes as a green tablet that turns a liquid blue as it dissolves. However, generic forms of the drug may not contain this dye.

Users can swallow Rohypnol caplets or crush them into a powder. The powder may be snorted or dissolved in a liquid and drunk or injected. Nicknames for Rohypnol include circles, forget-me pills, la rocha, Mexican Valium, R2, roach, and roofies. The drug has become popular at clubs and festivals because it is relatively cheap. In addition, many users mistakenly think the

Illegal Rohypnol is a problem everywhere. In one bust, police in Finland confiscated about 400,000 Rohypnol pills and the materials to make 1 million more.

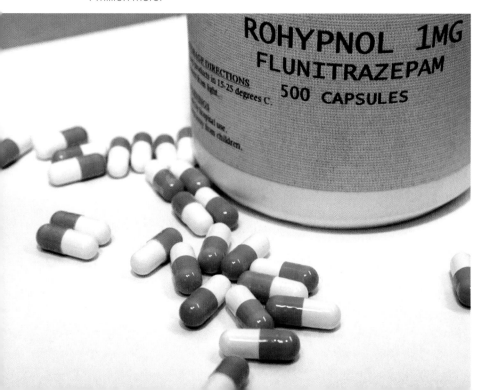

drug is safe because it is manufactured by a pharmaceutical company rather than produced in illicit labs. Some people take the drug to counteract the effects of stimulants such as cocaine.

ROHYPNOL EFFECTS

Rohypnol begins to take effect within 15 to 20 minutes. The effects can last 12 hours or longer. Like GHB, Rohypnol binds to GABA receptors, causing feelings of relaxation, drowsiness, and decreased anxiety. Rohypnol can also result in impaired judgment, confusion, memory problems, slurred speech, weakness, lack of coordination, and headaches. Occasionally, it can cause the opposite effects, as some users become more excitable or aggressive after taking Rohypnol.

At high doses, Rohypnol can cause a person to lose consciousness. The drug may cause partial amnesia, in which a person forgets everything that happened while on the drug. An overdose of Rohypnol, especially if combined with the use of another depressant such as alcohol or heroin, can lead to coma or slowed heart rate and breathing, sometimes leading to death.

Long-term Rohypnol users may experience depression and difficulty thinking. Frequent users may develop tolerance and addiction. Those who stop using the drug may experience withdrawal symptoms, including headache, muscle pain, anxiety, restlessness, confusion, irritability, and hallucinations. In rare cases, someone who stops using Rohypnol may experience

AVOIDING DATE RAPE DRUGS

According to the National Institute on Drug Abuse, people can take several steps to avoid unknowingly being drugged with ketamine, GHB, or Rohypnol:

- Always pour your own beverage. Even people you know and trust might try to slip something into your drink.

- Never leave your beverage unattended, even if this means you have to bring it into the bathroom with you.

- Don't share drinks with others.

- Don't drink from punch bowls or other shared, open containers.

- Stay with your friends. If one of them starts acting dizzy, confused, or in another way that seems unusual, seek medical attention. If you feel intoxicated, ask a friend for help.

Some companies are also working to develop products that can detect whether a drink has been spiked with certain drugs. In the future, stores may sell nail polish that changes color if dipped in a drink containing a date rape drug. Or, straws or drink coasters may detect the presence of drugs.

seizures or heart failure. Rohypnol withdrawal should be overseen by a doctor, who can lower the dose over time.

KETAMINE, GHB, ROHYPNOL, AND SEXUAL ASSAULT

Ketamine, GHB, and Rohypnol are sometimes referred to as date rape drugs because of their widespread use in sexual assaults. At clubs or parties, predators may slip these difficult-to-detect drugs into unsuspecting victims' drinks. People under the influence of these drugs may become confused or easily influenced. They may experience physical weakness or difficulty moving, making it difficult to resist an assault. In some cases, they may fall asleep or become comatose, making it impossible to fight

Some date rape drugs dissolve quickly in liquids. Many are colorless, odorless, or tasteless.

back against an assailant. Because these drugs cause memory problems, the victim may not remember the details of the assault the next day, making it difficult to report the crime.

Ketamine, GHB, and Rohypnol also make users vulnerable to other crimes, such as robbery. The last thing victims of these crimes may remember is accepting a drink from a stranger. The next thing they remember is waking up with all of their money gone.

INHALANTS

Inhalants are fumes from substances such as glue, spray paint, nail polish remover, and cleaning fluids. Some people inhale, or sniff, these substances to get the feeling of being high. The chemicals found in these products include toluene, butane, benzene, hexane, acetone, methanol, isopropane, and others. The chemicals in inhalants are toxic and deprive the brain of oxygen. They can damage the brain and other organs in the body.

Because inhalants are common household items, they are easy to find, making them frequent substances of abuse among young people. Inhalant use

Fumes from spray paint and other chemicals can make you sick. ▶

is also called volatile substance use or solvent use. Some users refer to it as huffing. Common street names for various types of inhalants include laughing gas, snappers, poppers, bold, and rush.

TYPES OF INHALANTS

NIDA separates inhalants into four categories: solvents, aerosol sprays, gases, and nitrites. Solvents are liquids that become gases at room temperature. Examples of solvents include dry-cleaning fluids, gasoline, correction fluids, felt-tip marker fluid, paint thinners and removers, glue, and lighter fluid. Solvents are inhaled by soaking rags in the liquid and breathing through the rag. A person can also pour the liquid into a cup and breathe the fumes as they rise from it.

Aerosols are substances that contain both a solvent and a propellant, or a compressed gas that expels the contents of a can. Aerosols include spray paints, vegetable oil sprays, computer cleaning products, hair spray, and spray deodorants. Users may spray the aerosol into their nose or mouth. Or, they may spray it into a bag and then hold the bag to their face to sniff it.

Gases can be found in both household products and medical settings. Household products containing gases include butane lighters, propane tanks, and whipped cream dispensers. In the medical field, the gas nitrous oxide is used as a short-lasting anesthetic. When used as a club drug, nitrous oxide comes in cylinders, balloons, or aerosol cans. Users inhale directly from these containers. Nitrous oxide is colorless, odorless, and sweet tasting.

In the 1700s, theaters in London, England, offered people nitrous oxide, also known as laughing gas, to inhale for entertainment.

Nitrous oxide is often used in dental clinics.

Inhalants such as nitrous oxide, which comes in small canisters or balloons, are popular at music festivals and raves.

Nitrites were once used for chest pain and are still sometimes used in the medical field. But the Consumer Product Safety Commission banned their use in household items. Even so, they are sold illicitly, labeled as leather cleaner or room odorizer. They often come in glass vials, which users break to inhale the fumes from the liquid inside.

In some states, minors cannot buy household products containing potential inhalants.

INHALANT EFFECTS

The effects of inhalants are felt immediately but last only a few minutes. This may lead users to inhale the substances repeatedly, often for hours at a time.

When people breathe in inhalants, the fumes are absorbed through the lungs and enter the bloodstream. Once in the blood, the chemicals make their way to the brain and cause intoxication. Almost all inhalants—aside from nitrites—act as depressants. They produce effects similar to those of alcohol. Users may feel happy and relaxed. Some people say they feel as if they are floating through the air when they use inhalants. Breathing in nitrous oxide can cause hallucinations, giddiness, and exhilaration. Other symptoms include dizziness, lack of coordination, slurred speech, slowed thinking and movement, blurred vision, and tremors. Some inhalants cause headache, nausea, and weakness. Using inhalants can damage the heart and immune system, the body system that helps protect against diseases. Solvents can cause breathing issues and pneumonia.

"Tomorrow is the sixth anniversary of our son Justin's death. He was sixteen. He died from inhaling air freshener, an act of inhalant abuse. His senseless death rocked the worlds of all who knew him. Justin was an honors student who loved life and embraced it with enthusiasm. . . . I will always be haunted by the question of whether Justin would be with us today had he known about the risks he was taking."[2]

—Jackie, parent

Inhalants can cause sudden sniffing death syndrome. This occurs when inhalant sniffing causes the heart to develop rapid and irregular rhythms, causing cardiac arrest. A person can die the first time he or she uses an inhalant. Users who repeatedly sniff inhalants can die from asphyxiation as the chemicals replace

oxygen in the lungs. Some users suffocate when they place plastic bags over their heads to inhale fumes.

LONG-TERM EFFECTS

Long-term use of inhalants has been shown to damage the liver and brain and lead to kidney failure. Some users experience nerve damage that may lead to difficulty walking or talking. Brain damage can also result from inhalant use, making it difficult for people to learn new things or to participate in conversations. The chemical benzene, found in some solvents, can stop bone marrow production. This can lead to a form of cancer called leukemia. Inhalant use has also been connected to depression, suicide, binge drinking, and impaired memory. Long-term memory issues have repeatedly been found in studies of inhalant use.

In some people, inhalant abuse can lead to addiction. Withdrawal symptoms may include tiredness, nausea, weight gain, and seizures.

DESTROYING MYELIN

Myelin is a fatty tissue that surrounds many of the body's neurons. It provides a layer of protection for the neurons and also helps them carry messages quickly between the brain and the body. But long-term inhalant use can damage myelin. This can disrupt the nerves' communication system, leading to muscle spasms or tremors. The effect of inhalants on myelin is similar to that of multiple sclerosis, a disease that destroys myelin and causes muscle incoordination and weakness.

EFFECTS OF INHALANTS

SIGNS OF INHALANT ABUSE

If someone is using inhalants, friends or family may notice several warning signs, including:

- Dry and irritated skin or sores around the mouth and nose where the fumes make contact during inhalation
- Frequent nosebleeds or runny nose
- Frostbite or burns
- Red or watery eyes
- Breath that smells like chemicals
- Paint or stains on the body or clothing
- Hidden cans of empty paint or other chemicals
- Acting drunk or dizzy
- Loss of appetite
- Anxiety or irritability

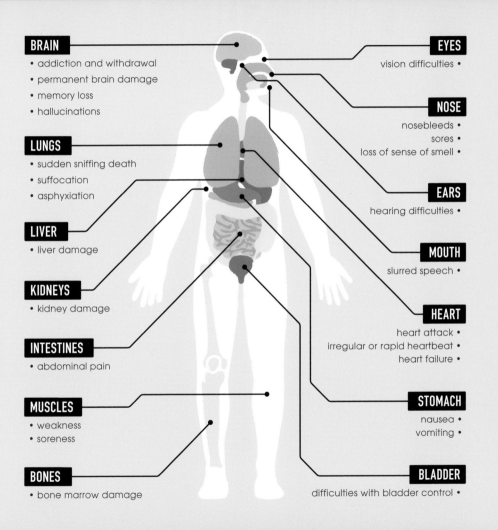

BRAIN
- addiction and withdrawal
- permanent brain damage
- memory loss
- hallucinations

LUNGS
- sudden sniffing death
- suffocation
- asphyxiation

LIVER
- liver damage

KIDNEYS
- kidney damage

INTESTINES
- abdominal pain

MUSCLES
- weakness
- soreness

BONES
- bone marrow damage

EYES
vision difficulties •

NOSE
nosebleeds •
sores •
loss of sense of smell •

EARS
hearing difficulties •

MOUTH
slurred speech •

HEART
heart attack •
irregular or rapid heartbeat •
heart failure •

STOMACH
nausea •
vomiting •

BLADDER
difficulties with bladder control •

CLUB DRUGS AND SOCIETY

According to NIDA, drug abuse costs the United States more than $740 billion a year in crime, lost productivity, and health care.[1] While the majority of this cost is related to tobacco and alcohol and drugs such as heroin, prescription opioids, and cocaine, the abuse of club drugs takes a toll on society as well.

SCHOOL, WORK, AND LIFE

Club drugs can affect the way the brain functions, especially in young people whose brains are still developing. This can hurt users' grades, college placement, and future job prospects. In addition, under the influence of drugs, young people's judgment

may be impaired, leading them to make poor choices, taking risks or having sexual contact they would not otherwise consent to.

Among adults, club drug abuse can affect work performance. Employees who regularly abuse drugs tend to produce lower-quality work and complete less of it. They may disrupt their coworkers' work too. If they come to work under the influence of drugs, they may pose a danger to the safety of other workers, especially if their job involves operating heavy machinery. Some employees even steal from employers to get money to buy drugs.

DRUGS AND MENTAL HEALTH

According to studies, drug abuse and mental disorders are often comorbid. That is, they occur in the same person at the same time. This does not necessarily mean that one causes the other. In some cases, a person with a mental health disorder may abuse drugs in an effort to self-medicate, or ease their symptoms. In other cases, use of a drug may trigger or worsen a mental health disorder in someone already vulnerable to that disorder. The most common mental disorders include anxiety and depression.

People with these disorders are twice as likely to abuse drugs or alcohol as others.

Teens are especially vulnerable to co-occurring drug abuse and mental disorders. Most mental illnesses, including anxiety and depression, first develop during adolescence. This is also the time when many people first experiment with drugs. Changes in the brain during adolescence may make young users more likely to develop addiction or other mental disorders after using drugs. Those at greater risk for substance abuse may also be at greater risk for suicide.

IMPACT ON THE HEALTH-CARE SYSTEM

Club drugs can also have an enormous impact on the health-care system, especially when taken by large numbers of people at raves and music festivals. During these events, hospitals are often overwhelmed by an influx of young, severely ill patients. During the July 2017 Hard Summer music festival in Los Angeles, for example, 49 people were sent by ambulance to local emergency rooms. And in 2013, 22 people were sent to the hospital during the Electric Zoo festival in New York City. Two of them died, and another five had to be placed into intensive care. According to Dr. Philip Fagan, director of the emergency department of Good Samaritan Hospital in Los Angeles, people may become ill at other types of events as well, but other events do not cause such high numbers of life-threatening emergencies among young

Increases in patient numbers due to drug overdoses can stretch emergency room staff beyond what they can handle.

people. "We don't have as many people that are comatose and medically compromised," he said. "I don't know anybody dying at USC [University of Southern California] football games from drugs and alcohol."[3]

Possession of MDMA can lead to a jail term of six months to 15 years, depending on the state in which the offense occurs.

The sudden arrival of so many patients can stretch a hospital's resources, making it

difficult to treat other patients. At one hospital, for example, 28 of 50 emergency room beds were occupied by rave attendees at one time. That left only 22 beds for people suffering from other emergencies.[4] In addition, patients who are not comatose may not cooperate with doctors. Police officers and staff members may have to hold them down to administer treatment, potentially endangering themselves and others.

IMPACT ON LAW ENFORCEMENT

Drug use is also often linked to crime. It is a crime to possess, manufacture, or sell drugs. In addition, drug use is often connected to violent crimes, including sexual assault. Law enforcement has a strong presence at many raves, often making arrests related to drug use and sales. In 2013, police at the five-day Lightning in a Bottle music festival in Los Angeles arrested 58 people on drug charges.[5] Most were arrested for drug sales—even if they gave their drugs away for free, which is also illegal.

Other law enforcement efforts are direct toward stopping illegal drug manufacturing and trafficking. According to the US Department of Justice, most of the illicit MDMA in the United States is smuggled into the country from Canada or Mexico. In June 2017, border police stopped a couple transporting 53 pounds (24 kg) of MDMA from Canada to the United States.[6] The pills had a street value of $880,000.[7] Police

SILK ROAD

Silk Road was a website that existed on the dark web, an encrypted portion of the internet that contains many illicit sites. Silk Road sold illegal drugs. Users could purchase any drug they wanted from sellers and have it shipped to their homes. Purchases had to be paid for with Bitcoins, a form of digital money. Federal Bureau of Investigation (FBI) records indicated that Silk Road processed 1.2 million transactions between February 2011 and July 2013.[8] The FBI arrested the website's owner, Ross Ulbricht, on October 1, 2013, and shut down Silk Road. But other online drug marketplaces have appeared in the wake of Silk Road's closing.

have also worked to shut down labs in the United States that illegally produced MDMA, GHB, LSD, and other illicit substances.

FAKE DRUGS

The emergence of designer drugs, also known as novel psychoactive substances (NPS), in recent years has made enforcing drug laws more difficult. Designer drugs are created in a laboratory to mimic the effects of illegal substances. Because these drugs are similar but not identical in chemical structure to illegal drugs, they are often difficult to regulate. It is easy, and often cheap, to order NPS from other countries and ship them to the United States. Often, they are labeled as research chemicals. Although it is illegal to sell analogs, or substances derived from illegal drugs, in the United States, manufacturers often label these substances as not intended for human consumption, making their sale technically legal. In addition, some of the substances differ enough from the original drugs that they do not fall under existing drug regulations in many countries.

BIG MONEY

Manufacturing and trafficking club drugs is big business. In October 2017, police in Malaysia seized 560 pounds (254 kg) of ketamine worth an estimated $3 million.[9] In February 2017, police in the Netherlands seized 100 bottles of hydrogen gas, 33,069 pounds (15,000 kg) of caustic soda, and 793 gallons (3,000 L) of other raw materials, all intended to manufacture MDMA. Officials said there was enough material to make one billion MDMA pills.[10] Those pills could have sold for up to $45 billion.[11]

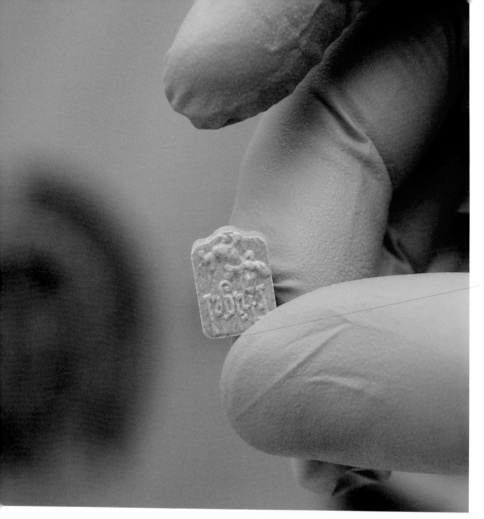

Club drugs are a problem around the world. MDMA tablets like this were imported to Colombia inside beer cans from Europe.

"They are psychoactive drugs sold under false pretenses, often as household products," explains Michael Baumann, head of Designer Drug Research at NIDA. "This is purely to skirt regulation."[12]

NPS produce many of the same effects as MDMA, LSD, ketamine, marijuana, and other drugs. Sometimes these drugs are sold as the drugs they are intended to mimic. But they often cause unwanted and unexpected side effects. According to journalist Nicola Davison, making even the "tiniest molecular tweak can create a drug with dramatically different psychoactive effects."[13] For example, the designer drug methoxetamine is often sold as ketamine. Like ketamine, it can cause dissociative effects. But it can also cause anxiety, paranoia, diarrhea, nausea, vomiting, and difficulty breathing. Other NPS include bath salts, which mimic the effects of MDMA, and NBOMe, often sold as LSD.

The number of NPS entering the market increases every year. According to the United Nations Office on Drugs and Crime, an average of 100 new designer drugs are developed every year. Between 2009 and 2016, 739 novel psychoactive substances were reported in 106 countries.[14] By the time authorities identify and outlaw one substance, a new one has often entered the market.

DRUG ANALOGS

Although drug analogs are also illegal, it can be difficult to prove that a substance is an analog of a drug. To be considered an analog of an illegal drug, a substance must meet three criteria:

- The new substance must clearly be intended for human consumption. Authorities can prove this by showing that the drug has no legitimate industrial or other purpose.

- The drug must be structurally similar to an existing illegal drug. This can be proven using scientific instruments that examine the chemical structure of a substance.

- The new substance must cause the same reactions in the brain as an existing illegal drug. Researchers test this using rat brains.

CHAPTER NINE

PREVENTING CLUB DRUG ABUSE

Many people feel that the costs associated with club drug abuse—including death—are too high. But people disagree about how to deal with the problem. Some believe the focus should be on preventing drug use. Others would like to ban raves and other events where the use of club drugs is common. Still others think the focus needs to be not on stopping drug use but on making it safer.

PREVENTION EDUCATION

Many federal, state, and local organizations are dedicated to preventing drug abuse before it starts. Many drug prevention

Through programs such as DARE, police officers educate middle school students about the dangers of drugs. Many believe middle school is the most crucial time to begin drug education.

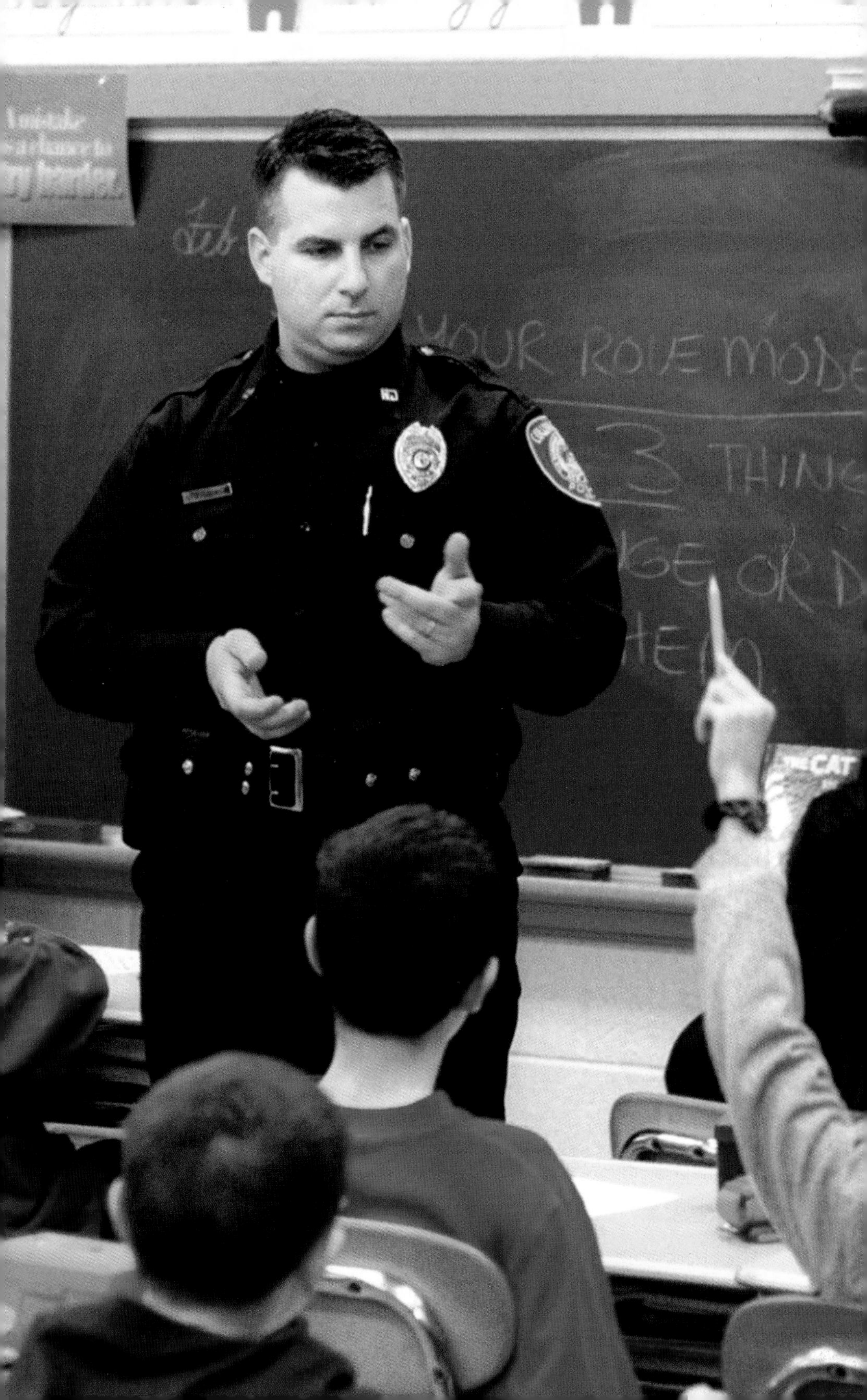
YOUR ROLE

Raves can be held indoors, but they are often crowded and hot.

programs target middle school students. These programs focus not only on the dangers of drugs but also on how to resist peer pressure to use drugs. One of the most widely used prevention programs around the world is Drug Abuse Resistance Education (DARE), through which police officers visit schools to talk with students about drug use. Today, 75 percent of US schools utilize the DARE program.[1] Other drug prevention programs include Students Taught Awareness and Resistance (STAR), Life Skills Training (LST), and Prevention Dimension. According to

NIDA, for every dollar spent on drug prevention education, the country saves up to seven dollars in drug-related costs to law enforcement and health and addiction treatment.[2]

ENDING RAVES

Some people feel that drug prevention education isn't enough. They would like to outlaw raves and other events known for rampant drug use. In Los Angeles, for example, after several young people died at raves, a number of emergency room

DRUG TESTING

In addition to utilizing prevention programs to stop drug use, some schools employ random drug tests. These tests can be given to any student who participates in competitive extracurricular activities. Typical tests screen for marijuana, cocaine, opioids, amphetamines, and PCP. But if schools suspect students of using other drugs, such as MDMA or GHB, they can order tests for these substances as well. In addition, parents concerned that their children may be abusing drugs can use home drug tests to detect a number of substances. Some tests require a urine sample, while others involve simply wiping a surface their child may have touched.

doctors called for a ban on the events. According to Dr. Marc Futernick, the culture of such events encourages drug use. "Maybe it's the lack of supervision . . . maybe it's poor security at the door, maybe it's the culture of that's what you do at a rave—the only reason you go and listen to this electronic music is when you're really high on Ecstasy."[3]

Doctors also pointed out that raves pose particular risks because they are often hot and overcrowded, and they often last for hours. Attendees may be dancing out in the sun all day. This can be dangerous, especially when combined with drugs such as MDMA that can raise body temperatures. The huge crowds also make it hard to notice someone in medical trouble until it is too late. "Most people who are there don't know each other, they come from far away, they don't look out for each other," said Dr. Brian Johnston of White Memorial Medical Center in Los Angeles. "And as they do the drugs, they become

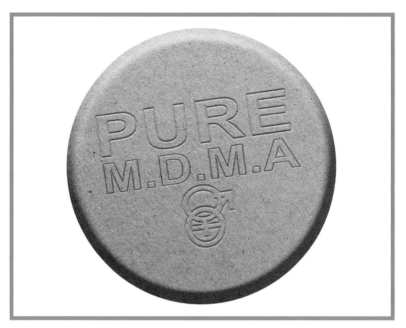

Just because someone claims that a drug is pure doesn't mean that it is true.

less observant, less capable of helping someone, less capable of recognizing someone who is in trouble."[4]

Because of the dangers associated with raves, some locations, such as the Los Angeles Memorial Coliseum, have stopped hosting them. But raves can bring large profits, leading other venues to continue to allow them.

HARM REDUCTION

Some people believe that rather than ending drug use, banning raves would actually make drug

"We believe 'raves' offer positive benefits to society, encouraging creativity, providing jobs to local artists and cultivating the values of empathy, peace, and unity amongst event attendees who then carry those values back into our local communities."[5]

—Petition by EDM festival fans

use more dangerous. According to Missi Woolridge of DanceSafe, "Banning EDM events won't stop drug use. It will only make drug-taking more risky by pushing it into the underground."[6]

Most of the world's illicit MDMA supply is produced in illegal laboratories in the Netherlands and Belgium.

Instead of banning raves, organizations such as DanceSafe want to employ a strategy known as harm reduction. Proponents of harm reduction believe that since some people will continue to use drugs no matter what, drug use should be made as safe as possible. DanceSafe, a group based in Denver, Colorado, sets up tents at raves and festivals to provide

Some music festivals set up tents with water, electrolytes, and medical aid, as they anticipate having to help people who have taken illicit drugs.

drug safety information. In some cases, the organization also provides free drug testing to let attendees know what substances are in their drugs. The tests produce immediate results, but they can only detect the presence of some drugs. In addition, they cannot tell how strong the drugs are. Proponents of drug testing say that it keeps people from accidentally ingesting substances they did not intend to take. For example, if someone purchased a drug sold as Molly but learned that it instead contained LSD or bath salts, he or she might choose to throw the substance away rather than use it.

DanceSafe wants to test drugs at US music festivals, as many European festivals do. However, few American festivals allow such testing. They are afraid that doing so would give the appearance of promoting the use of illegal drugs. According to Pasquele Rotella of Insomniac Events, an entertainment company that produces many raves, "Some people view partnering with DanceSafe as endorsing drug use rather than keeping people safe, and that can prevent producers from getting locations and organizing events."[7]

Other harm reduction groups, such as Conscious Crew, walk around raves and festivals looking for partiers who may need

"People get very squeamish talking about (drug education). But if you have someone who is determined to take this substance, would you rather tell them the safe recreational dose versus, 'well, just don't do it?' And then, they're going to go off and do something ignorant? That's where the problem is."[8]

—Stefanie Jones, Drug Policy Alliance

medical attention. They call emergency services when needed and stay with the person until help arrives.

In addition, some raves provide free water, misters, or air-conditioned cool down rooms where people can go to cool off when they get too hot. Some also provide public service announcements assuring people in attendance that they will not get into trouble with law enforcement if they need medical help for themselves or a friend as a result of drug use. In addition, some have set a minimum age requirement of 18 years for rave attendees.

THE RAVE ACT

In 2003, the US government passed the Illicit Drug Anti-Proliferation Act of 2003. It was originally known as the Reducing Americans' Vulnerability to Ecstasy (RAVE) Act. The act states that authorities can shut down clubs and fine owners large sums of money if people are using drugs at these events. The fines of $250,000 or more are enough to permanently close down businesses. Some people feel the RAVE Act has made raves less safe because owners are afraid to provide harm reduction services, such as free water or cool areas for attendees, out of fear that such actions will be seen as promoting drug use.

CLUB DRUG LEGALIZATION

Some people take harm reduction a step further and say that the best way to ensure that currently illegal substances can be used safely is to legalize all drugs. They say that it is not the drugs themselves but drug laws that cause problems. If drugs were legal, there would be no need for a black market to sell them, so there would be no profit for those who produce and traffic illicit drugs. In addition, there would be no incentive for illicit drug manufacturers to create new, unknown drugs to skirt drug regulations. Instead, people could purchase pure, clearly labeled drugs in specific dosages.

Others argue that legalizing drugs would result in a huge supply of dangerous substances. They would be cheaper and easier to obtain, meaning that more people would use them, leading to more health issues and a higher death rate.

According to the authors of the Monitoring the Future survey, no matter what happens with drug laws, "The drug problem is not an enemy that can be vanquished. It is more a recurring and relapsing public health problem that must be contained to the extent possible. Therefore, it is a problem that requires an ongoing, dynamic response."[9] As old drugs become popular again and new ones continue to appear, that response will need to change and adapt. But it will continue to center on warning young people about the dangers of drugs.

ESSENTIAL FACTS

EFFECTS ON THE BODY

- LSD: blurred vision, hallucinations, feelings of openness and trust, nausea, numbness, trembling, muscle weakness

- Other hallucinogens: relaxation, visual changes, mood changes, difficulty thinking, hallucinations, out-of-body experiences, increased heart rate and blood pressure, nausea, vomiting

- MDMA: feelings of openness and sociability, increased energy and confidence, muscles cramping, nausea, vomiting, teeth clenching, elevated body temperature sometimes leading to death

- Ketamine: disorientation, memory problems, hallucinations, out-of-body experiences

- Inhalants: dizziness, lack of coordination, euphoria, slurred speech, slowed thinking and movement, blurred vision, tremors, organ damage, cancer, death from sudden sniffing death syndrome

LAWS AND POLICIES

LSD, MDMA, psilocybin, peyote, and DMT are classified as Schedule I drugs. That means they have no medical value and are considered highly addictive. Ketamine is a Schedule III drug because it has medical value and is considered to be low to moderate in addiction potential. Inhalants are not scheduled drugs because they are fumes from legal substances.

IMPACT ON SOCIETY

Club drugs are often manufactured illegally within the United States or smuggled into the country from illegal labs in other nations. Because the drugs are made illegally, they do not meet any quality control standards. Substances labeled as one drug may instead contain a number of other drugs and chemicals at unknown dosages. Club drugs are often taken by young people at raves or parties, where attendees may dance for hours in the heat. The heat, in combination with club drugs, can lead to death. Even those who survive club drug use may experience lasting memory and thinking problems. They may perform worse in school or at work.

QUOTE

"Kids are being used as guinea pigs. The manufacturer didn't go through clinical trials, the person who orders and repackages it doesn't know what it's gonna do to somebody, and the user didn't know what it was going to do to them."

—*DEA spokesperson Joseph Moses*

GLOSSARY

BONE MARROW
Tissue inside bones where blood cells are formed.

CENTRAL NERVOUS SYSTEM
The brain and spinal cord, which transmit sensory and motor impulses through the body.

CONCENTRATION
The proportion of a specific substance or ingredient in relation to other ingredients.

HORMONE
A regulatory substance that sparks an action, such as growth, digestion, or sexual maturation, in a tissue or organ.

ILLICIT
Illegal or hidden.

INHIBITION
A mental restraint on a person's behavior or speech.

NARCOLEPSY
A disorder in which a person suddenly falls into a deep, brief sleep, even in the middle of the day or while performing other tasks.

OBSESSIVE-COMPULSIVE DISORDER
A psychological disorder in which a person feels the need to repeat certain words or tasks, to the point that it impairs everyday functioning.

PANIC ATTACK
Sudden feelings of intense anxiety and fear, often with increased heart rate, shortness of breath, sweating, and trembling.

POST-TRAUMATIC STRESS DISORDER
A mental health condition brought on by a traumatic event and usually characterized by irritability, anxiety, depression, and insomnia.

RECREATIONAL
Done to bring about feelings of pleasure or intoxication.

STIMULANT
A category of drug that affects the nervous system and increases the body's heart rate and blood pressure.

SYNTHETIC
Something made by combining chemicals, typically to imitate a natural product.

TUBERCULOSIS
An infectious disease of the lungs that can cause chest pain, fever, weight loss, and difficulty breathing.

WITHDRAWAL
The act of stopping use of a drug; the physical and mental side effects that occur when someone stops using a drug.

SELECTED BIBLIOGRAPHY

Drug Abuse Sourcebook. Detroit: Omnigraphics, 2016. Print.

Gahlinger, Paul. *Illegal Drugs: A Complete Guide to Their History, Chemistry, Use, and Abuse*. New York: Penguin, 2004. Print.

Kuhn, Cynthia, Scott Swartzwelder, and Wilkie Wilson. *Buzzed: The Straight Facts about the Most Used and Abused Drugs from Alcohol to Ecstasy*. New York: Norton, 2014. Print.

Liska, Ken. *Drugs and the Human Body with Implications for Society*. Upper Saddle River, NJ: Pearson Prentice Hall, 2009. Print.

FURTHER READINGS

Bodden, Valerie. *Club and Prescription Drug Abuse*. Minneapolis: Abdo, 2015. Print.

Bodden, Valerie. *Prescription and Over-the-Counter Drugs*. Minneapolis: Abdo, 2018. Print.

ONLINE RESOURCES

To learn more about club drugs, visit **abdobooklinks.com.** These links are routinely monitored and updated to provide the most current information available.

MORE INFORMATION

For more information on this subject, contact or visit the following organizations:

DEA MUSEUM

700 Army Navy Drive
Arlington, VA 22202
202-307-3463
https://deamuseum.org

Offering free admission, the DEA Museum seeks to educate the public on the history of drugs, addiction, and drug law enforcement in the United States.

MULTIDISCIPLINARY ASSOCIATION FOR PSYCHEDELIC STUDIES

1115 Mission Street
Santa Cruz, CA 95060-9989
831-429-6362
http://www.maps.org

This not-for-profit organization is dedicated to conducting research on hallucinogenic, or psychedelic, drugs such as LSD and psilocybin.

NATIONAL INSTITUTE ON DRUG ABUSE

6001 Executive Boulevard
Rockville, MD 20852
301-443-1124
https://www.drugabuse.gov

The National Institute on Drug Abuse is a government organization dedicated to advancing the study of drug use and addiction to improve public health.

SOURCE NOTES

CHAPTER 1. CLUB DRUGS IN REAL LIFE

1. Rong-Gong Lin II. "Three Who Died after Hard Summer Rave Overdosed on Ecstasy, Coroner Says." *Los Angeles Times*. Los Angeles Times, 30 Nov. 2016. Web. 18 Dec. 2017.

2. Rong-Gong Lin II and Matt Hamilton. "'I Tried to Do CPR and Nothing Was Working': 3 Die after Attending Hard Summer Rave near Fontana." *Los Angeles Times*. Los Angeles Times, 2 Aug. 2016. Web. 12 Feb. 2018.

3. Martin Robinson and Mario Ledwith. "'Where Am I, Where Am I?': Last Words of Nick Cave's Son Arthur, 15, Before He Fell 60ft to His Death from a Cliff after 'Freaking Out' When He Took LSD, Inquest Hears." *Daily Mail*. Associated Newspapers Ltd., 10 Nov. 2015. Web. 18 Dec. 2017.

4. "Montana Sean Brown, 15, 25I-NBOMe." *Just Think Twice*. United States Government Drug Enforcement Administration, n.d. Web. 18 Dec. 2017.

5. Patil Armenian and Roy R. Gerona. "The Electric Kool-Aid NBOMe Test: LC-TOF/MS Confirmed 2c-c-nbome (25C) Intoxication at Burning Man." *American Journal of Emergency Medicine Journal*. Elsevier, 26 Apr. 2014. Web. 28 Mar. 2018.

6. Carolyn Doherty. "Aria Doherty (Age 13)." *Alliance for Consumer Education*. Alliance for Consumer Education, n.d. Web. 18 Dec. 2017.

7. Sydney Lupkin. "Molly: Why the Club Drug Is So Dangerous." *ABC News*. ABC News Network, 23 Feb. 2015. Web. 18 Dec. 2017.

CHAPTER 2. CLUB DRUG HISTORY AND USE

1. Tom Shroder. "'Apparently Useless': The Accidental Discovery of LSD." *The Atlantic*. The Atlantic, 9 Sept. 2014. Web. 19 Dec. 2017.

2. Shroder, "'Apparently Useless': The Accidental Discovery of LSD."

3. Paul Gahlinger. *Illegal Drugs: A Complete Guide to Their History, Chemistry, Use, and Abuse*. New York: Penguin, 2004. Print. 43.

4. Shroder, "'Apparently Useless': The Accidental Discovery of LSD."

5. Shroder, "'Apparently Useless': The Accidental Discovery of LSD."

6. "LSD: A Short History." *Foundation for a Drug-Free World*. Foundation for a Drug-Free World, n.d. Web. 19 Dec. 2017.

7. Miles Corwin. "Psychiatrists Defend New Street Drug for Therapy." *Los Angeles Times*. Los Angeles Times, 27 May 1985. Web. 28 Mar. 2018.

8. "LSD: A Short History."

9. "Results from the 2015 National Survey on Drug Use and Health: Detailed Tables." *Substance Abuse and Mental Health Services Administration*. Substance Abuse and Mental Health Services Administration, 8 Sept. 2016. Web. 19 Dec. 2017.

10. Lloyd D. Johnston, Patrick M. O'Malley, Richard A. Miech, Jerald G. Bachman, and John E. Schulenberg. "2016 Overview: Key Findings on Adolescent Drug Use." *Monitoring the Future*. National Institute on Drug Abuse, 2017. Web. 28 Mar. 2018.

11. Johnston, O'Malley, Miech, Bachman, and Schulenberg, "2016 Overview: Key Findings on Adolescent Drug Use."

12. Colin Lecher. "What Drugs You Like Depends on Where You Go Dancing [Infographic]." *Popular Science*. Popular Science, 19 Apr. 2013. Web. 12 Feb. 2018.

13. Johnston, O'Malley, Miech, Bachman, and Schulenberg, "2016 Overview: Key Findings on Adolescent Drug Use."

14. "Results from the 2015 National Survey on Drug Use and Health: Detailed Tables."

15. Johnston, O'Malley, Miech, Bachman, and Schulenberg, "2016 Overview: Key Findings on Adolescent Drug Use."

16. Johnston, O'Malley, Miech, Bachman, and Schulenberg, "2016 Overview: Key Findings on Adolescent Drug Use."

CHAPTER 3. LSD

1. Ken Liska. *Drugs and the Human Body with Implications for Society*. Upper Saddle River, NJ: Pearson Prentice Hall, 2009. Print. 301.

CHAPTER 4. OTHER HALLUCINOGENS

1. Jan van Amsterdam, Antoon Opperhuizen, and Wim van den Brink. "Harm Potential of Magic Mushroom Use: A Review." *Regulatory Toxicology and Pharmacology*. Volume 59, Issue 3. Amsterdam, Netherlands: Elsevier, 2011. Print. 425.

2. Paul Gahlinger. *Illegal Drugs: A Complete Guide to Their History, Chemistry, Use, and Abuse*. New York: Penguin, 2004. Print. 273.

3. Gahlinger, *Illegal Drugs*, 404.

4. Gahlinger, *Illegal Drugs*, 411.

CHAPTER 5. MDMA

1. Peter Hess. "Partiers Confused about Ecstasy and Molly Confound Rates of US Drug Use." *Inverse*. Inverse, 24 Oct. 2017. Web. 20 Dec. 2017.

2. "Amphetamine, Methamphetamine, and MDMA—Production and Precursors." *European Monitoring Centre for Drugs and Drug Addiction*. European Monitoring Centre for Drugs and Drug Addiction, n.d. Web. 20 Dec. 2017.

3. "What Are the Effects of MDMA?" *National Institute on Drug Abuse*. National Institute on Drug Abuse, Oct. 2017. Web. 20 Dec. 2017.

4. "Emergency Department Data." *Substance Abuse and Mental Health Services Administration*. Substance Abuse and Mental Health Services Administration, n.d. Web. 26 Dec. 2017.

5. Rong-Gong Lin II. "ER Doctors: Drug-Fueled Raves Too Dangerous and Should Be Banned." *Los Angeles Times*. Los Angeles Times, 10 Aug. 2015. Web. 20 Dec. 2017.

6. Suzannah Weiss. "When Does Sex on MDMA Count as Rape?" *Vice*. Vice Media LLC, 24 Aug. 2017. Web. 20 Dec. 2017.

7. Weiss, "When Does Sex on MDMA Count as Rape?"

8. "The Truth about Ecstasy." *Foundation for a Drug-Free World*. Foundation for a Drug-Free World, n.d. Web. 20 Dec. 2017.

9. Cynthia Kuhn, Scott Swartzwelder, and Wilkie Wilson. *Buzzed: The Straight Facts about the Most Used and Abused Drugs from Alcohol to Ecstasy*, 4th Ed. New York: W.W. Norton & Company, 2014. Print. 95.

10. Ben Sessa. "MDMA and PTSD Treatment: 'PTSD: From Novel Pathophysiology to Innovative Therapeutics.'" *Neuroscience Letters*. Volume 649. Amsterdam, Netherlands: Elsevier, 2017. Print. 178.

11. Peter Hess. "Hair Test Reveals All the Drugs Actually Hiding in Ecstasy Pills." *Inverse*. Inverse, 18 Sept. 2017. Web. 20 Dec. 2017.

SOURCE NOTES CONTINUED

CHAPTER 6. KETAMINE, GHB, AND ROHYPNOL

1. "K Cramps." *Onket*. Onket, n.d. Web. 21 Dec. 2017.

CHAPTER 7. INHALANTS

1. Brian E. Perron, Joseph E. Glass, Brian K. Ahmedani, Michael G. Vaughn, Daniel E. Roberts, and Li-Tzy Wu. 2011. "The Prevalence and Clinical Significance of Inhalant Withdrawal Symptoms among a National Sample." *Substance Abuse and Rehabilitation*. National Center for Biotechnology Information, 4 Apr. 2011. Web. 29 Mar. 2018.

2. "The Truth about Inhalants." *Foundation for a Drug-Free World*. Foundation for a Drug-Free World, n.d. Web. 21 Dec. 2017.

CHAPTER 8. CLUB DRUGS AND SOCIETY

1. "Trends & Statistics." *National Institute on Drug Abuse*. National Institute on Drug Abuse, n.d. Web. 22 Dec. 2017.

2. "The Truth about LSD." *Foundation for a Drug-Free World*. Foundation for a Drug-Free World, n.d. Web. 22 Dec. 2017.

3. Rong-Gong Lin II. "ER Doctors: Drug-Fueled Raves Too Dangerous and Should Be Banned." *Los Angeles Times*. Los Angeles Times, 10 Aug. 2015. Web. 20 Dec. 2017.

4. Lin, "ER Doctors: Drug-Fueled Raves Too Dangerous and Should Be Banned."

5. Katie Bain. "Was Lightning in a Bottle Unfairly Targeted by the Police?" *LA Weekly*. LA Weekly LP, 25 July 2013. Web. 22 Dec. 2017.

6. "53 Pounds of MDMA Found in Car Crossing US–BC Border." *CBC News*. CBC, 14 June 2017. Web. 22 Dec. 2017.

7. "US Border Protection Just Seized $880,000 in MDMA Coming from Canada." *Vice*. Vice LLC, 20 Nov. 2015. Web. 22 Dec. 2017.

8. Donna Leinwand Leger. "How FBI Brought Down Cyber-Underworld Site Silk Road." *USA Today*. USA Today, 21 Oct. 2013. Web. 29 Mar. 2018.

9. G. Surach and Ashwin Kumar. "NCID Makes Biggest Ketamine Bust of the Year at KLIA." *The Sun Daily*. Sun Media Corporation, 23 Oct. 2017. Web. 29 Oct. 2017.

10. Kara Fox. "Chemicals for One Billion Ecstasy Pills Seized in the Netherlands." *CNN*. Cable News Network, 10 Feb. 2017. Web. 22 Dec. 2017.

11. "Ecstasy: Discussion Guide." *PBS*. Public Broadcasting Service, n.d. Web. 22 Dec. 2017.

12. Erika Gebel Berg. "Designer Drug Detective Work." *Chemical & Engineering News*. American Chemical Society, 11 July 2016. Web. 22 Dec. 2017.

13. Kevin Loria. "One in 10 People around the World Gets High Off Designer Drugs." *Business Insider*. Business Insider Inc., 1 May 2015. Web. 22 Dec. 2017.

14. "Global Synthetic Drugs Assessment: Amphetamine-type Stimulants and New Psychoactive Substances." *United Nations Office on Drugs and Crime*. United Nations, 2017. Web. 29 Mar. 2018.

CHAPTER 9. PREVENTING CLUB DRUG ABUSE

1. "About D.A.R.E." *DARE*. DARE, n.d. Web. 22 Dec. 2017.

2. "Is Drug Addiction Treatment Worth Its Cost?" *Drug Abuse*. National Institute on Drug Abuse, n.d. Web. 29 Mar. 2018.

3. Rong-Gong Lin II. "ER Doctors: Drug-Fueled Raves Too Dangerous and Should Be Banned." *Los Angeles Times*. Los Angeles Times, 10 Aug. 2015. Web. 20 Dec. 2017.

4. Lin, "ER Doctors: Drug-Fueled Raves Too Dangerous and Should Be Banned."

5. Lin, "ER Doctors: Drug-Fueled Raves Too Dangerous and Should Be Banned."

6. Anna Condrea-Rado. "How Do We Stop Drug Deaths at Festivals?" *Vice*. Vice LLC, 17 Mar. 2017. Web. 22 Dec. 2017.

7. Condrea-Rado, "How Do We Stop Drug Deaths at Festivals?"

8. Condrea-Rado, "How Do We Stop Drug Deaths at Festivals?"

9. John Schulenberg, Lloyd Johnston, Patrick O'Malley, Jerald Bachman, Richard Miech, and Megan Patrick. *Monitoring the Future*. National Institute on Drug Abuse, July 2017. Web. 22 Dec. 2017.

INDEX

ABOUT THE AUTHOR

Cordelia T. Hawkins is a children's author and editor. She lives in Wisconsin.